EXCERPTS *from a*

SECRET PROPHECY

Joanna Klink

PENGUIN POETS

PENGUIN BOOKS

Published by the Penguin Group
Penguin Group (USA) LLC
375 Hudson Street
New York, New York 10014

USA | Canada | UK | Ireland | Australia | New Zealand | India | South Africa | China
penguin.com
A Penguin Random House Company

First published in Penguin Books 2015

"Askesis" by Jordan Konkol is reprinted by permission of the author.

LIBRARY OF CONGRESS CATALOGING-IN-PUBLICATION DATA
Klink, Joanna, 1969–
[Poems. Selections]
Excerpts from a secret prophecy / Joanna Klink.
pages ; cm.—(Poets, penguin)
ISBN 978-0-14-312687-4 (softcover)
I. Title.
PS3561.L5A6 2015
811'.54—dc23
2014045788

Printed in the United States of America
1   3   5   7   9   10   8   6   4   2

Set in ITC Galliard Std
Designed by Ginger Legato

for my parents, William and Judith Klink

ACKNOWLEDGMENTS

ACADEMY OF AMERICAN POETS   *Given, Pericardium, Stars, scatterstill*

A PUBLIC SPACE   *Elemental*

ARTS & ACADEME, THE CHRONICLE OF HIGHER EDUCATION   *The Graves (Wind for your sickness)*

BLACK WARRIOR REVIEW   *Early Night, Askew*

BOSTON REVIEW   *Aubade (Caravans of wind), Aubade (Who lives where summer ends), Novenary*

HARVARD REVIEW   *Aubade (What is one hour)*

H.O.W. JOURNAL   *Obituary, Terrebonne Bay (Before the hour when the coast), Terrebonne Bay (Leading into the bay)*

KENYON REVIEW   *Dream of Hands, The Graves (How many days?), The Graves (Sometimes on the steps), Night on Land, Noctilucent, Processional, Stillways*

NEW ENGLAND REVIEW   *Excerpts from a Secret Prophecy*

NEW REPUBLIC   *Terrebonne Bay (The deep evening-colored rose), Terrebonne Bay (The old vandals were floods and boats)*

PLOUGHSHARES   *The Graves (So here are the strange feelings)*

POETRY   *Toward what island-home am I moving*

SHARKPACK POETRY REVIEW ANNUAL   *Variations on a Trance*

SYCAMORE REVIEW   *Blizzard*

Grateful acknowledgment to The University of Montana, The Ucross Foundation, Civitella Ranieri, Jeannette Haien Ballard, Lannan Foundation, and The American Academy of Arts and Letters.

Paul Slovak, thank you. Thank you Mark Lane. And immense gratitude to my other readers: Patrick Hutchins, David Greenberg, John D'Agata, Amanda Fortini, David Baker, and Ken White.

My love to Prageeta Sharma, Dorothy Wang, Andy Laue, Nat Levtow, Candice Mancini, Antonia Wolf, Deb Busch, Saul Melman, Julie Rae O'Connor, Brian Chikwava, Mia Žnidarič, and Steve Klink.

CONTENTS

Now let us issue from the darkness of solitude.

Virginia Woolf, *The Waves*

EXCERPTS *from a*

SECRET PROPHECY

ELEMENTAL

I brought what I knew about the world to my daily life
and it failed me. I brought senseless accidents
and a depravity sprung inside the jaw.
Also I brought what I had learned of love,
an air of swift entrance and exit, a belief in trouble
and desire. It will amount to something
I was told, and I was told to hold fast to decency,
to be spotlit and confident. I was told
next year's words await another voice.
But you are a hard mouth to speak to
and if I write the list it will be free of constancy.
It will include fierce birds, false springs,
a few oil lamps that need quickly to be lit.
Also dusk and weeds and a sleep that permits
utter oblivion from our stranded century.
This is not a natural world, and if there are
recoveries from confusion, they pass like rains.
I don't look to the robins for solace; neither do I trust
that to make an end is to make a beginning.
If we are not capable of company, we can at least
both touch the quartet inside evening,
the snow inside the willow, the bewildering kinship
of ice and sky. But as I walked
I saw crows ripping at shapes on the street,
a square of sunlight flare on the roof.
Take my hand, if only here and not in the time
that remains for us to spend together.
We will stand and watch the most delicate weathers
move, second by second, through the grim neighborhood.
I will lean into you, who have loved me in your way,
knowing where you are and what you care for.

THE GRAVES

So here are the strange feelings that flicker
in you or anchor like weights in your eyes.
Turn back and you might undo them,
the way trees seem to float
free of themselves as they root.
A swan can hold itself on the gray ice water
and not waver, an open note upon which minor chords
blur and rest. But it was born dark.
The shore of that lake is littered with glass.
How you came to be who you are
was all unwinding, aimless on a bike,
off to retrieve a parcel that could only be a gift,
and felt, as a child, the sea
weave around your feet, white light rushing in with the surf.
What lived there?

        —Joy, dispatched from nowhere,
and no need to think about your purpose,
and no fear that the sun gliding down
might burn the earth it feeds. Black habitat of now
in which decimation looks tender.
Sometimes the call of a bird is so clear
it bruises my hands. At night, behind glass,
light empties out then fills a room and the people in it,
hovering around a fire, gorgeous shapes of wind
leaning close to each other in laughter.
From this distance, they are a grace,
an ache. The kingdom inside.

TOWARD WHAT ISLAND-HOME AM I MOVING

Toward what island-home am I moving,
not wanting to marry, nor wanting
too much of that emptiness at evening,
as when I walked through a field at dusk
and felt wide in the night.
And it was again the evening that drew me
back to the field where I was most alone,
compassed by stems and ruts,
no light of the fixed stars, no flashing in the eyes,
only heather pared by dry air, shedding
a small feathered radiance when I looked away,
an expanse whose deep sleep seemed an unending
warren I had been given, to carry out such tasks—
that I might find *nothing dead*.
And it was again the evening that drew me
back to the field where I could sense no boundary—
the smell of dry earth, cool arch of my neck, the darkness
entirely within myself.
And when I shut my eyes there was no one.
Only weeds in drifts of stillness, only
stalks and gliding sky.

Come, black anchor, let us not be harmed.
The deer leafing in the dark.
The old man at the table, unable to remember.
The children whose hunger is just hunger,
and never desire.

BLIZZARD
Two deer in the crosswalk

Who kept watch over their confusion
Who saw the snow vanish
   before touching the ground

Who kept watch when
having not fed its own
   people the town
turned ice-white

Snow fell that day as it falls
   constantly through sleep
lush drumming to nothing
waves of hard silver

Now it descends into the white
darkness of your privacy
   and you awake to the boreal
century that is yours

            Your rib-stick animals
            Your exhausted men

Wind woodsmoke and ice spilling
blind on the bird
   whose wings
blow lightly apart

On a man in a cotton jacket
   awake under
wet squares of cardboard

Who keeps watch when that wind
shocks the frozen parking-
    lot asphalt

        Have you come to buy bread
        Have you come to buy meat

Scarce living in the town that
now skims
    the lake of your
privacy where in summer you loll
on the slats of the jetty

And the long summer dusk
    your feet kicking up waves
A water now fully rock

Ice-sheet of the north, who peers
    under that surface
Who looks without blame
at the ones by the electric
    doors of the store

        Feels the far-flung cities of dawn
        Or wearies of suffering

You asked
to live among others
and here you are
    living

A snowflake is unlike a night-flying moth
The cabin by the lake is a shelter
    for your limbs
which are constantly warm

Concerning the white star
that sometimes flashes
above the snowy gray town
   I have heard
it will soon have no message

THE GRAVES

Sometimes on the steps you forget you are lasting
in sunlight. You forget kinship, as when,
through dusk, deer keep the color of the field.
You forget rest, and a room that fills—
a spare music, like bells. Sometimes red stars
appear in the ceiling's slight tear and there are times
I would add myself to that night sky, eerie and un-
touched. Waves of daylight and darkness protect against
nothing. Sometimes the aquifer rises into your eyes,
a mass of deep greens, ancient and mineral-
lustral. Undersea moons make patterns on the wall
and shape the hours you are not there.

           —There is a fine morning haze
that will not come to me. In the years left to me
I would change. The lights above a town
hold out a delicate blinking whiteness,
however small, and my skin comes to them,
a loom of burrs. If I belong within stillness
the lanterns may answer, hung on branches
that, caught by wind, sound like the pulling-away of waves.
Even trees hold their frames when the wind rips through them.

OBITUARY

I was dry moon and tide. I was half of the sea's
        being-asleep. Wearing a wool skirt
under the soak of sun all summer I heard,
through the shudder and fever, something falling.
        A dead tree.
        The heart of a fish in a trap.

The sea made a bouquet of the reeds,
a dress of the gulls. Still there was some
miscalculation in the nearby untouched
        grassland, in the dawn's
smoke-faint folding of hands.

High in my chest that razor-pressure
        dissolved, the way in northern forests boreal lakes
        bleed apart. I did not heed
anything enough. I don't know
if my wounds were wounds to the eyes
or the heart. When they looked away,
        I also was included
        in the contents of mirrors.

I saw, within stillness, every depth of twilight.
And when the hard veins broke from my wrist—
        summer rains
        opened there.

*

When you loved did you plot?
When you spoke what did you hear?
Were you among those who,
      like the moon, draw close to the earth.
You who once looked out of my eyes.
You who, matter-of-fact, swept the forest
                 in spines of fire—

Your song came only to this:
through the dusk and immensity
blood-muscle, blood-loved, turning the soil
      into cloud, the cloud
into fields, the black
      grass-chill at morning.

There is a bone forever unmoved in your throat,
your body windburnt,
your dreams absentminded and huge.
I think your sadness was beautiful
      in its way, when you were with us.

TERREBONNE BAY

THE DEEP EVENING-COLORED ROSE of the sea
is closing. Sweet crude oil, orange as rust,
finds an open pathway into the marsh.
And what you thought would be your home,
lush with grasses, is no home, drives you out into the gray-glazed
gates of sleep. Blood flowers
where we don't see it. And every chance event
is a high note racing from stars in sea-depths of brightness,
and every shock we feel we feel only with the slack
ropes of our arms. Someone
wants to hide the body of oil and cannot.
Someone wants to hide their hands from shame.
Shark, dolphin, manatee, fish,
each slick skin an undreamt tine threading its red
flute-dusk through fumes.
Sound of the flood-dark pulse.
Then the second when the water makes no sound.

THE OLD VANDALS WERE FLOODS AND BOATS
eroding the banks. The islands that once dotted the bays
have sunk, disappearing into silverish grit, thinned
into algae and filament now being made
quiet by plumes. Despite ourselves
we are made quiet. The death of the sea
a thing we must lower ourselves into
to imagine. I will stay with you here
inside the sheen of orange that quickly kills,
not like the saltwater slowly starving the freshwater-
marshes and grasses that knit this green-wet
world together. The two breathless gannets
found covered in oil are not unlike you,
at the mercy of a mercy that moves in plumes,
that insists certain fates remain
invisible. What existed before the oil arrived
was delicate and mired, a broom of moonlight
swept through half-choked waves. I trust you
if you wish for what it, too, might have been.

LEADING INTO THE BAY are soft green expanses of
grasses, saltwater channels, slicks
not glimpsed here before.
The birds bathe where they can,
in half-damp shadows that make possible the next free
climb into air. There is nothing beyond our means to feel it—
oil pushing up to the surface where the surface-dwellers die,
turtles pulling in from the Gulf for nesting.
If I close my eyes I can hear the faint blue
traces of blood over-gathered by oil
and the sound of ice near the seafloor.

There will be a time when nothing living moves,
a degradation of stillness beyond any liquid scar.
Still, the solutions of despair are weak
if you believe you can touch an undersea reef,
the belly of a small wounded whale.
You have the power to feel it.
The breath of the animal
moving like trust into your arms.

BEFORE THE HOUR WHEN THE COAST slid into ocean
we thought we saw a patch of sun greening in waves.
The slip of a fish. There was a need
so deep in our bodies we could not even weep.
We called for an end and that end
did not come. Power after power, our machine tools
and cutting tools did nothing to hold back the brown clouds
rippling in chaotic columns toward the light.
And what the skies mean, passing over beds of tarred
seaweed, feels unutterable, like the darkness
around a candle. Where had we hoped to live?
You came into the month with dreams.
You walked on those beaches even though
you knew they were sick. The bird that sought
the reeds to die in, the fish gill-soaked with oils—
you gathered them into yourself as if you alone
could bring back their flickering.
And overhead the novae exploded toward you
along tracks of gas and dust, and the fields of ocean
rose into you, and the crabs broke from their cancer fossils
in masses of tiny flowers and you felt inside you
the islands re-arise, flushed from the thickening
imbalance of the earth. (Is there some
refuge beyond ourselves that is vast enough?
The sea is without grief. As are the days.)

THE GRAVES

Wind for your sickness.
The moon for your sickness.

      A river of night-
      trees. Mossy patches

where something recently slept.
A hand-drawn sketch of
fish for your sickness,

      red and ghost-
      loamed. From your mother,

for your sickness, a late
flock of snow geese
swept up in a gust.

      From your father, a cave
      of violas in luminous
      pitch. For the panic

desolation. For scratchy bed-
sheets, the gathering of tumors,
a dispensation traveling in

      farnesses across the
      galaxy-quiet of what is

to come. Dark-sunned,
you are swimming in schools.

      For the despairing quality of
      hospital fluorescence,

the secondhand alarm—
theft of time theft of

      hope. The messages
      arrive like flowers.

For the common un-
contested light of dusk.
For tobacco moths

      in clouds of wings at
      the door. For the dawn-

emotion, a calm-in-vastness
that descends upon
what is. Upon the storm-

      tangle of branches, wing-
      veins and hand-veins
      shadow-shown on that pale

skin of sky. Too stone for
fear. Too brittle for

      findings. From the powers that,
      born on the site of sorrow,

fall in strands of smoke
across your sickness,
for your sickness,

      and carry and keep you.
      That would keep you here.

NOVENARY

River. Riverline of moon.
Along the bank, crows dragging their wings,
a black seam.

You curve inward, miles from any landmark,
aurulent hunger for some other
course. Painstakingly
amassed. Proof of quiet, in aria.

The stillways come to you,
sable-blued in the burnishing dark.

*

Nine fish below the surface, phosphorescent.
Nine important stars.
Night in its full summitry, as if I'd been waiting
for years. The small of my back
hollowing to slope under the dress.

I came here to be opened,
the way a telescope, wavering, discovers then dwells.
Nine winds lifting up from the slow current.
Nine rumors of load-bearing sleep.

*

What can you shed of yourself,
keeping store against time.
November's black sky scored with dust, ice,
though it has not yet snowed.

Is this a response to the dark
that can hold. Above the floodplains of sleep,
a few trees crowd with moon-lanterns.

Are the thoughts running through my body
any different.

They see and shine by night.

*

Night, place of peace. Could I lean any further
into your silk-folding surfaces, drawn out
to no place I know. Am I a factor
in your nightly spindrift, the cold nets of fire

that, vanishing, pass through you.
Skeleton-sound of moving water, silt-awash.
Could I too grow luminous in tapering,
apprentice myself to senescence,

as if my body had always been
intended to be this blind shell.
Taste of smoke at the bay-mouth,
where phosphor endlessly burns.

If there is rarity in me, signal the course.

*

Where my life, hollowed out by solitude,
kept me from sleep, I scoured the reed-roots,
the sanded eyes of the crows.
Under a dry moon I kept company

with augury, felt alert to threat.
These are seasons, not eternities,
but to live here, thin water and candor,
is to be stranded. Autumn, morning, dusk,

I scoured the river, opal-alluvial.
I wanted to know and I wanted to ask.

If I am only hull to what happens,
let me at least feel more deeply that flitting,
the dead light of stars over my hands,

into my throat. Oar of my body.
Such things as were sensed but not known.

ISLAND STATES (NIGHT-SHINING)

There was no beginning,
no fierce ancestry blown into place,
no headlights making glow a few feet of road.
Backward in my mind a soft breeze flew,
shadows peeling for a second from the leaves that
    gave them shape.
I knew every signal, every disapproval—
in the house, each was its own keeper of rules.
Devotion like the old-growth forests, ancient,
    implicit.
I knew every occasion—the music rising off the piano,
held in the air in plumes of distraction, sometimes rich,
    sometimes scaled to terror—
nothing in the rooms that was spacious or small.
No one slept; truly no one greeted you without a smile.
I practiced instruments, practiced living in days
stripped of complaint—because what use is complaint
when you've been given everything you need to keep alive?
No sounds dark enough to jolt us open.

I welcomed the spring-gray clouds, darts of rain
on the wide window-glass, a silence hinting at *this*
    or at *here*. And when the old clock stopped,
when thunder cuffed the attic and a bird slipped into sky—
that was the music,
that was poetry's brief spell of blue light declaring
    We are disappearing
    There is great love here
    There is great ruin.

And I might have heard in the diminishment that followed
a voice asking if you could ever travel
far enough if you tried. And thought it said

You don't have to carry on quietly,
don't have to believe there is something
    worth going back for.
You don't have to know if you are thirsty
    or full, or if you even wish to drink.
But believe in the night-shining music
that gathers up, in fine glints of breath against
    glass, every one
who helped you and brought you this far.
They cannot know what it meant.

GIVEN

And I carried to that emptiness
between us the birds
that had been calling out

      all night. I carried an old
      bicycle, a warm meal,
      some time to talk.

I would have brought
them to you sooner
but was afraid your own

      hopelessness would keep you
      crouched there. If you spring up,
      let it not be against me

but like a weed or a
fountain. I grant you
the hard spine of your

      childhood. I grant you
      the frowning arc of this morning.
      If I could I would give you

a bright throat and even
brighter eyes, this whole hill
of olive trees, its

calmness of purpose.
Let me not forget
ever what I owe you.

I have loved the love
you felt for those gardens
and I would grant you

the always steadying
presence of seeds.
I bring to that trouble

between us a bell that might
blur into air. I bring the woods
and a sense of what lives there.

Like you, I turn to sunlight for
answers. Like you, I am
not sure where it has gone.

EARLY NIGHT, ASKEW

When you ask   *Why such indignation*
at violation   the screen door slams again

Because there was nothing clean in it
no honor to defend   except privacy

that peculiar stiff gaze   more rote than meaning
her knees knocking her into the dusk

Why such nonchalance   Why the strident
vellum voice now that the guise of camaraderie

belongs to sharp daylight
What is remarkable   What is improbable

What is shameless or feckless or vague
I would keep my own counsel

and the paper cuts on my hands
would skin over   the dull bolt

fanning across my left temple   Darkness
seems to be folding itself into this town

like subterranean brume   smudges
on the shop-glass   people as they pass

nodding to each other   Early moon
I can hardly understand

One might have hoped for less
less damage   less smugness   Even now

you seem to me monstrous
So that surely you must speak and act

from some vastly erased chamber
Preening   lumbering

Do you struggle   to see yourself clearly
One might start with the givens

Birds glide through dense forests
at evening   saplings silver over

To watch this happen is to make oneself
part of the mud-bed   the jigsaw

the constant awkward jostling of things
If we stand ourselves   deep in that woods

at night   there will eventually be a concert
Some mornings   fern dust

small wobbly bees   who scratch when they land
To have vista means to see the dead ships

as seed-stars   the nettles as corals
be dumbfounded

only as long as rashness permits
There may be something inside you

that is polished   zealous
in two Junes I could shoo you away

But when you reached your arms
out into the night   you needed   like me

an answer   and the low-flying geese
brushed the air over the lake   and were gone

VARIATIONS ON A TRANCE

Robins in the cottonwoods,
holding still as the thin snow comes.
The sun seems to flood them with blood.
They have settled in the empty branches
while the storm-lamps spit in your limbs,
red evening swinging across the sky then dropping,
ragged, into your frame to stay with you
as you move and smile and have opinions.
Then a woman's torso white with dawn—
their rich perch is yours, there is nothing you need
to expect or retrieve, like warm fields
floating toward an invisible moon.
A person learns stone-throated composures
and barters for days of calm weather,
like a man in a dream who understands the answering
pressure of eyes—you ask too much.
But the birds are not reckless.
Every minute their fat shapes are filling with sun,
and I apprentice myself to their candor.
Their bodies drift on the moving branches, solid—
they are not taking and keeping.
They are not torn papers in a rumor of wind,
their small backs brown fields holding thunderclouds up.
Inside their bodies, nothing falls to the earth and dies.

AUBADE

CARAVANS OF WIND, a cast-over
starlessness. Is the brunt
of taking leave mine,

> whole nights vanishing again
> into the crass dailiness of
> morning.

Ends-of-summers ends-of-
towns. You pull
back into the truce you've

> made with yourself.
> Four shades of white.
> Never time for the precision in

limbs, languor, the slower
charge where your eyes

> release into mine to feel
> the slight weight and
> shift. Ground

in spring and its dark
pressure of flowers.
Instead the sudden fever-

> mark on my cheek,
> a sharp heat that
> flies from your

palm as you press it
for a second where my

heart under skin is. Hive-in-
ivory. Is it this traction,

      is it the rampant property-of-
      night we share and see,

at the gravesides every day
as we are talking with someone or
sitting or just staring

      out. Water in the color of
      daylight. Whose are you
      in that intense and separate
      ache if not mine.

WHAT IS ONE HOUR
that I should care
that I should lose him again.

    We are each of us faraway
    animals, steadfast in our

inner ardors, midnight's
fretted distress under a thin

    moon. *Lechuza*, for hours
    trunk-rapt in stillness, raises its

loaded wings, shedding
nacre over the lake.

    You saw it too, air
    and silver, a current of
    muscle curving through

space in its wake, blood
underflown in your ribs.
How to explain it never

    happened and was *this real*,
    screech owl or simple
    barn, one of the great

shadows moving inside
wind, wars loves disease and
chances, the malaise of

ingratitude, arsenal of material
energies and medicine
to the stricken, all striving-

until-death crushed and
laced again into patterns of

sound, road-dusted or sand-
marshed, and the long slow

summer of creek water,
summer of high old trees
moving the light—all of it

in the quick flint-struck
fire we trade the next
day in our eyes.

WHO LIVES WHERE SUMMER
ENDS knows the hard cold of

      autumn is blissfully
      close, although it feels
      each season newly un-

known. You are constantly
newly unknown to me,
my night-glowing openhearted

      sting-of-salt weather.
      Rains and winds, sleights of
      hand. Who if not you

could weigh me down.
You'd paint my eyes
blacker and warmer than they are

      and soon they would carry
      whole calendars of
      black night in them.

Maybe you think you trade
one clean joy for

      another. But mine is darker,
      slanted, nitrous blue at the

root. To be another
person than the one

you were before means
more than I understand.

But my hands
move in streams
over you whether you travel or not,

as you drop into sleep or not,
and in the book of this
most-alone-place I am

there only when you feel
need, a coat so thin and so like

skin you can touch the
slopes, the smoother

pools, dust-mooded
winds over roads, the skeleton
instrument of your voice

as it richens the maps
and paths, summer's last
shades of white on dark soil,

as if the moon-moth and
house-mouth were

close against the lashes
of your eyes, puzzles-in-
flutter, or wandering

off through the warm night air,
unlikely ever again to find
such light as this.

PERICARDIUM

Am I not alone, as I thought I was, as I thought
The day was, the hour I walked into, morning
When I felt night fly from my chest where prospect had
Slackened, and close itself off, understanding, as I thought I did,
That the ground would resist my legs and not let them
Break nor let them be released into air as my heart, in its
Muscle, might be released from the body that surrounds it,
Like someone who, placing a hand on a shoulder's
Blade, felt a life move inside an hour and a day
Break from the day the hour meant something more than weakness,
More than fear, and flew forward into the depths of
Prospect, your arms, where you'd been, before me, waiting
For me, the way the body has always been waiting for the heart to sense
It is housed, it is needed, it will not be harmed.

STILLWAYS

Except in darkness a fog has brushed against grass

Except a rain moving through branches at night
        has lifted away: from the window
        you watch but don't see

Except in spring there are days when the shawl of snow
        has sunk into earth

and the grass beads with fog-dust
        and you have slept, and when you woke
            found that nothing had
            changed

And set out into the lead-lights of dawn,
        your travel quiet, eyes half-
        closed to the cold

as the corridors of night spread out before me
        in that narrow morning, and I thought I heard voices calling
            as the light came on—

But there were no voices, there was no message

Nothing but rain-dust and moth-dust

Nothing but the sound of rain
        papering a few
        leaves at the edge of
        the field, making
        inside me a hollow
        chronicle of blood,

tissue, some formless
transparency—

and later I thought I heard rain drum in the fireplace,
                        the soft pulse
                        scattering—

So all of this need not have happened

So the future surrenders again

And everything that bears happening
        cannot happen again

Whether a heartbeat

Whether a child

Whether something simply growing inside you
                at a slower pace, too slow
                for this life, an oar
                held above
                water, still and un-
                troubled, before heart-pull or
                pattern, prior to
                color

Whether, in the first hours of understanding, you walked out
        feeling the breath-task in all things
        entangled with rain

Terrain of minor stars, terrain of incomplete hunger—

I did not ask for it, but it came

And the distance separating us from the world of those
                          who have fully died—where
                          do we station
                          ourselves if we
                          want to draw
                          them back
                          enough to feel
                          their presence a little
                          longer

And the life that does not rise or follow

The expectation that hardens into a blind *what-you-want*
                          These are the plans I have
                          made for you these
                          are the hopes I
                          have for you here
                          is the character of that pain:
                          in any circumstance to *hold yourself still*

Whether the rain flecks down your face
          and the gray atrium of sky
          presses far too
          hard against your eyes

Whether the next blueprints, too, must be abandoned—
          the afternoon might bring sunlight

Could it bring an hour of sunlight

—who will I be?

And who will I have been if, daughterless, I fill out these remaining
                          minutes of my life.

*

Heat lightning, dusty roads,
      jeans, I was born between
      farmlands that were never mine.

Fireflies across the sloping yard little hoodwinks
                        of dusk.

I would burrow you into the crux of my arm
      but for the sorrow I might find there.

Call to me across the calcium dirt, the blood-
      root of one hundred worn acres,
      and I will find my way to you.

Under the ravine of evening
      are stream banks, strips of resin,
            a new moon.

Landscape with no nickname or origin.

Water swinging over carpets of plate glass.

*

To be empty and clear about who you are

To back off the exaggerations

Understanding the world will not meet your desires
         but offers up such hazards as might
                        alter you

Think of the fog in the grass that won't burn away

Think of the blurred warmth of sleeping skin,
         the tiny bones that might have
         grown there:
         you feel but don't see

And, century to century, how many near-presences
                        have formed in the tamped
                        centers of bodies
                        like clouds of light that
                        vanish in the clear
                        air above fields, grieved
                        and unspoken

Does the silence as it widens
         have no purchase

Will expectation and regret consume us

And the cloud-scraps of moon and the endless
                        moon-calculations:
                        you see but don't know

whether the future you talk about is *yours*

or also belongs to those around you
         who gain and lose something each day

And, like wind lifting across gray mud
                        the rain, grief
                        grows voiceless—

all our lives moving toward that boundary
as if disappearing from who we
might be—

And the field I walked to with its stillness,

That place with its stillness,
whose inward keep
is our dark
privilege. The love you feel for what you've lost.

3 BEWILDERED LANDSCAPES

NO PAILS, NO MOONS. No apology for the forest that is not numinous. The gates of evening open out to nerves blood and bone. How raw can you become. These are the tactics and half-measures of an insomniac world. No body wrapped in the thick peace of sleep, no flow of current when one star goes out. There was always certainty in isolation—wood stone and grass. But for the frailty of my body it helped to know I was alone. The fireboats sped over water, the water filmed with old stars. Nothing more than the pitch of the wind through some slanted dead tree. Nightly I opened and closed, magnetic with hope. No stone now to show me the path. No grass without the once-rich color of sea. If there is a way, let it be without having and losing. No pails to carry. No waves to pour out or free.

I DO NOT RECOGNIZE MY LIFE. There is no being-born, no aura of coves, no boat to speed me past this anchorless plane— no homeward-coursed forward-flight. The beams of light overhead in a forest pure and aloof. What would they have me do. Can you alter the scope of your own loneliness. Can you touch one thing that will not vanish. Nightly the shift of an island, the inaudible barge floating past. If you hear me, come quietly. I would not lose my hold on this delicate earth.

STARS, SCATTERSTILL. Constellations of people and quiet.

Those nights when nothing catches, nothing also is artless.

I walked for hours in those forests, my legs a canvas of scratches,

trading on the old hopes—*we were meant to be lost.* But being lost

means not knowing what it means. Inside the meadow is the grass,

rich with darkness. Inside the grass is the wish to be rooted, inside the rain

the wish to dissolve. What you think you live for you may not live for.

One star goes out. One breath lifts inside a crow inside a field.

REPORT ON FIRE

City of dawn. City of trails of trash.
Men in makeshift overcoats blur
slowly by. Up close they move like ghosts
and from a distance the gray rain
sparks on the boarded-up windows.
And no one that day even wished to
speak about it. I didn't say a word
but heard the even beating of heart
beneath a hunger so wild and constant
the heart itself seemed like nothing.

If I reach for you whom I love most,
with your wry smile, your body's depth-of-warmth,
I can forget their hunger.
Still, the elaborations of loss run
parallel to our privacies, a land-in-flame
we never have to see, whose smoke we recognize—
and only when it is impossible to breathe
are we prompted to partial fury—our own air!
Across the fields a sudden cold
clears the smoke, the gray lakes stitched by winds.
We may be spared by weather.
But that other world still tries to breathe.

And it seemed that in a while this world
would temper us, blur its spiking edges.
Scraps of ice in snow that falls
as if to make all gray things white—
a few exposed pipes, street-side litter, high-rises
for miles. And for a time you could imagine
each life behind each window, however old,
however injured, standing and moving
as if through many rooms where food
had been prepared, and heat given.

And there is a stillness washed into certain winds
at certain hours, and a flow of power
that flashes in sunlight through black winter-bleached
trees. It hardly staves off vanishing.
Nor is it mine, writing *Joanna* on the scenes
that flood my head in the dark.
From this low station of quiet, however much
I cannot see or understand, I do sense
the impress of birds on the sky as they lift, mid-city,
from their aching branches, or catch the dusk
as it separates from fog and snow and blurred car-lights—
the spread of movement along night,
a fold of breath in each element—
and the barely-lit figures, exhausted, headed home,
and the others holding back, still holding on.
The light of fountains passing through their bodies.

Are there people you should shut out?
You would go mad *every day*.
The shadow cast by earth fills with
black blood and blue nerves.
There are gestures so small they seem like
nothing—to catch someone's eyes and find
beneath the scorn a maze of need.
What did our lives mean.

THE GRAVES

What was falling so steadily, so slowly
we did not notice—the land covered in summer
then, before we knew it, scored with fire and flood,
a dream we tried uselessly to squint through.

Once we felt a great calm cross the field
until flocks rose in curves into night's
slow vault—answering to the summons that said,
before we even knew what it meant, *attend*.

We come into the world with black-adapted eyes.
Hundreds of years of rain abandoning itself
to the cities and far tracts of grain.
Even the greenest city may become a reef.
Take nothing more from each other.

NIGHT ON LAND

It must have seemed a long
time to you, evenings and
nights, breath by

      breath, year by year, wind
      on the bridge sweeping
      away the soak of dusk

so that the sky rose in white
corridors of light
above us. Moving water

      below. I know you can neither
      hear me nor understand,
      caught as you are in circuits of

doubt, and the river we crossed
most evenings, there and back,
can't help you beyond

      marking time that has
      passed and keeps passing.
      So much hardship

and exposure undertaken
together and one day it's gone.
Please you say, as if the throat

      knew the next word.
      Who would stay here,
      knowing we won't swear

anything to each other.
Night takes nothing
from us, the river a descending

       scale of quiet, terrestrial,
       blackening each rock to water—
       and the fish that barely

flash when they dart into
their crude corners.
If this is the beginning, again,

       of solitude, is there no way
       for you to accompany me
       through the long hours

ahead, the familiar patter of
faint house-sounds.
Love, which should run deep,

       thins into evening, wears us
       back, wears us down,
       and what seemed brave in our

turning to each other now seems
small, a safeguard or
distraction against

       disappointment. But I think
       you were really next to me
       in warmth, by my side

in the refuge of daily life, shirt
wallet shoes, a walk to dinner
over the river, your thoughts

well within my own—and laughter
and the absentminded way we
moved through our days, sturdy,

steady—gone before we had
the chance to see what it meant
or could mean, night on the bridge

or night on land, your arms around
my waist, sorry and hasty, asking
nothing more than hope.

EXCERPTS FROM A SECRET PROPHECY

No one knew how to live there   merciless mid-
Atlantic heat   grime on the hot car windows
and trash-heaps along schoolyards   we went
to neighborhood markets for collards
Saturday   the humidity at 9 a.m. already un-
bearable   in grooves down our cheeks
rough trust   that we wouldn't have to stay
make a home there   never a grand
city at night where blue-sooted evenings
you could stand on the sidewalk   and look in

Windows fire-bled so that figures at meals
seemed to rise in gray radiance

Who looks inside   says less and less
the years abandoning their force I remember
black shades of red wine   the books I could barely
afford   twice a day to the library
homeless men asleep by its pillars afternoon
rains in Baltimore   dark blue
against the energy at work in my head

And so often in the afternoons I have felt this
strange mental life   curving   separate
as if my blood were iron   the storms
arriving in patterns of lush thunder
a cool spray   spun back from the grass

Once I lived throatless   believed that
holding back sorrow would make sorrow
soften   So easy to place an X
over who you were   the soil under rain

now the fires shifting plates
beneath this wet cement

And if I have hoped for more
it is only the whole of loneliness
swept away by understanding

*

Who were you then   wanting to learn
reading all day all night   fall in a strange city
year after year   No one knew what to tell me
keep studying   through the bay window sirens
and the silences that followed   snow blurring down
to the sick city trees   walking to campus hi hello
the women in Italian boots for seminars
4 hours later   at the crosswalk you saw
no one you knew

You greet each person on the street   and the dark
civilization of wind slams through you

*

No one knew what was coming   miscarriage
divorce disease   the country at war   air
brightening and darkening around the notebooks
I hauled wherever I went   was I meant
to understand then how little I would
matter to the future   I spent winters

summers   trying to see   driving out to the horse farms
poplars lining the road   pools of sunlight sinking into
fields   the air darkening how long
can you wait   your body crowded over with
clouds and grasses   whole childhoods of grain blown
back and forth inside your eyes

*

I waited a long time   to find you
late in my life   homesick for nothing I could
recognize   another winter in an eastern city
iron grates dusting over with snow   quiet cells
at night undetected   forgettable by dawn
Still I watched you place your hand   against the window's
ice-burned sheet   and trace wet stars that
rose in ghostly lines during the city's
night-slowed snowfall   warehouses
leaping to your touch roughed in brick

Your eyes   everything worth striving for
to be what you saw   There were times
with you   burning through skin marrow shadow night
after night   what you brought to my body when we agreed on
silence I never imagined   such closeness

Despite the terrible predictions   we drove to the coast
minus 10 and the beach was frozen   pressed
transparent ice against our eyes
And nobody stood with us   troubled by the ocean materials
oily debris   carcasses of sea fish languishing
frozen by the iced seaweed   a kind of tundra we crossed

as though   had we kept moving a   creature might simply
turn alive   the gulls huddling in their slicked
wings for heat   our lungs
draining   filling with ice air

And the wide stillness
where the gull-cries should have been

*

Place an X over who you were
it doesn't help   Shut your eyes there are
abrasions beneath the eyelids   Coming to understand
the ones you most love will die   out here
I can feel the weight of the sky   the evening
turning black its arid grasses

You changed who I was   around you I felt
the need for pattern a physical need
to bring the hard light of the stars
inside   it never worked   Under this moon
the mountains ripple in moth-thinness
they would be crushed if you touched them
and the old oaks bracing the street   the theater
whose placard is half-stitched by frost   are nerve-endings
where the sting of being-alive   can't stay captured

Night-watcher   Pillar   Winters
passed   iridescent ice
filming on the lake   the water caught in
merciful shades of white

The lines were cut deeply by skaters
I moved   the words in my head
trying to say what it has meant

*

So much yours I hardly saw what was
happening to me   give yourself like that
and you are sure to lose something
Holding up all the beams of a life   you paced along
bookshelves   smoked constantly   nicotine
arching through the cranial vault   the same one
splendid with thoughts   some days whitening to
disarray   Who looks inside says   less and less
I felt   below the blue-brown seasons of snow
the desiccated grooves of branches   something
shift   my love   leaving you

Spring pre-spring   an increase in pests
and parasites   plants blooming too early
I let it fall apart   and when it did
couldn't understand   what was being asked of me

Spring rains refilling the aquifer all summer
alone again   orange cat sprawled across
the dictionary   standing at the window
night after night remembering the prairies
where I was born   under deep lakes of cloud
It didn't help   nothing helped
No one knew what to tell me   keep living

*

How long can I wait   What I say
today and what I say tomorrow   perish equally
I loved you   but have already forgotten
how it felt   perhaps a joy   that came in droves

Out here   you can hear everything at night
a dog in the distance calling out for company
someone slamming a door   Just to stay
and not be drawn forward   light
in the afternoons   slowly sailing into pines

I have tried   to be both *open* and *among*
and find myself always moored by
inner anchors

But most hopes are private and flicker
between burdens we can't share

Perhaps   like the wooden rains that drop across
this valley   you are drawn to stillness
perhaps like me   you are clearing a space
inside you   a floor where everything might spill
The clouds above these ridges   show no hint
of any cause   Night   falls again
we river into one another   not understanding
how much debt we owe   to those we pass on the street
Like you   I would have done things differently
would have held on longer   The world
breaks   is always breaking   our bodies
bear tremendous sorrow and still
we stay as long as we can

DREAM OF HANDS

Skies over fields, hatch-marks of rain. Rich smoke lifting from

Plain haylike things. When night fell again the eerie flute-call

Of the elk felt like an arc of coins across a sky so emptied of light

Your own arms seemed remote. From such depths and such heights

We cross through our lives, belonging to patterns that surge

And recede. Falling bricks in our dreams, the piano-practice of hands—

The light coming through curtains, the light going out. Leaves

Making black shadow-shapes on the grass until one hour of wind

Clears them away. The loss of people in a single minute

On earth. We have no human voice that can stay long enough

To see anything but rising, subsiding. Today you were spared.

On a train platform, a woman bends down to her child. In a glass building

An elevator shoots, imperceptibly, into the high void of steel.

NOCTILUCENT

Not only the roads. Not only the streamwater,
raw, against my face and hands.
Not the painstaking ground faith that has kept me
   here, the nerves and reeds
rooting down to alluvial soil, reaching far below earth to the ruined
   starwork. I was alone.
Not only the tarnish, the tiny lettering from the firelit
   world that is dawn. Spoken for as I was
spoken for—climbing for years from that place.
Not even an hour. Not even an obscure
pathway to day, a road washed with dust, and the passerines
in their winding tapestry above it, flung toward immeasurable
   islands of light. Trees, lookouts,
the insides of things streaks of blue—you arrived and I watched you.
No longer capsized in sleep. Or by night at the window,
   trapping heat on the glass—skin
over the heart. Unable to lessen the darkness.
Until you brought me, casually, an hour.
And not only an hour—a night, a night.
   The still light of lakes. The notes floating free of their sheets.
Not only the moods, the rooms, a prediction of flowers—
   the seeds and the plans. But my body
lifting and plunging, up the stairway of blood,
   hard into your arms—
however much I had wanted to leave the world briefly,
   just for a moment—a barely measurable time—
no longer those fields in half-smoke through twilight,
no longer the snow blown across roads,
and the winds that seem to pick us up
then toss us down, not even the clocks, not even the watches,
the acreage, the farmers and tourists, the faraway
   stone ports of call,
those inner sea-worlds and the outer clouds,

the rains appointing the oceans, the ships forcing past docks,
and the algae glowing blue inside the black bay,
    vanishing, lustrous, and the mornings
where I find you with me again, free in the arch of your torso,
and all the mornings that were not given to me
that are now given to me, for no reason I understand,
and the light that falls over us in sheets of slow
quiet—uncountable, undreamed, even in the lesser
    minutes of my life, which I now would
keep, and hold close, if only for you.

THE GRAVES

How many days? Days we arrive at evening
not knowing their meaning. For a moment

your hand catching the bone of my hip
filled our aloneness, but the orders inside stayed

shut. Sunlight flew through the air
and we hovered, felt age in our skin like a thick

indoor dusk. Foolhardy to think the syllabary
would soon catch fire and plunge its message

into us. I believe I am here. I know something
beats inside the seasons and will close up to view

if I try to use it. Never-ending countries—
a whistle from the street, scalding coffee at dawn,

two hundred tiny birds lifting effortlessly
from the oak. And that red darkness rising into wind,

the coffins arriving off camera at Dover
under cover of night. I am only a field-ghost,

a routine of sleep and labor and unwinding.
But would keep my eyes wild enough to feel

those bodies blinking in me—all too unsteady,
the earth, not on our terms but moving to

meet us. (And certain griefs cannot be brought inside,
too full as they are of their own destinations.)

Merciful that it is possible to sleep with such
ancient harm taking constant place around us,

taking each thing away from you and then life itself.
Vital force branching through my lungs, my hands, shine—

please shine—if what we are meant to be is more than this,
more than the hours coming upon us in the dark.

PROCESSIONAL

If there is a world, let me be in it.
Let fires arise and pass. The sky fill with evening air
then sink across the woodlots and porches,
the streams thinning to creeks.
In winter there will be creatures half-locked in ice,
storms blown through iron grates, a drug of whitest ardor.
Let the old hopes be made new.
Let stacks of clouds blacken if they have to
but never let the people in this town go hungry.
Never let them fear cold. If there is a world,
let it not be temporary, like these vague stars.
Let us die when we must. And spinelessness
not overtake us, and privation,
let rain bead across tangled lavender plants.
If there is a world where we feel very little,
let it not be our world. Let worth be worth
and energy action—let blood fly up to the surface skin.
If you are fierce, if you are cynical, halfhearted, pained—
I would sit with you awhile, or walk next to you,
and when we take leave of each other after so many years,
the oaks will toss their branches in wheels of wind
above us—as if it had mattered, all of it,
every second. If there is a world.

NOTES

ELEMENTAL

"For last year's words belong to last year's language
And next year's words await another voice.

[. . .] And to make an end is to make a beginning."

—T. S. Eliot, "Little Gidding"

TERREBONNE BAY

"BP agreed to plead guilty today to charges of manslaughter, environmental crimes, and lying to Congress in connection with the 2010 Deepwater Horizon drilling rig explosion, which killed 11 workers and sent as much as 200 million gallons of oil into the Gulf of Mexico." —*ProPublica*, November 15, 2012

ISLAND STATES (NIGHT-SHINING)

This poem responds to, and is indebted to, Jordan Konkol's poem "Askesis," *Colorado Review* 41.

ASKESIS

It began in a room like this.
I was at first upright,
I knew the walls and loved them;
no voice challenged that estimation
or demanded my revision or sacrifice.
I knew every wall; it began with music.
The keys were the teeth
of the infinite lock. My hands
were the keys to every door; I was there.

Of course it goes wrong for everyone,
doesn't it? Unravels, counting down, skyward.
I studied the film. A practice of negation
I've learned should be systematic,
intentional, temporary.
Though one manual advised *even periods* of silence.
I had been so cloaked in it that when
the harsh light ripped open a bird (frost)
on a walk, from nowhere—that was poetry,
that was the god's gift. How I wish I knew then
it could be pure, as everything is, unearned & pure,
like dawn—could be the pearl this field
encloses. That it was and is every thing, my body,

the voice saying you don't have to write, don't
have to revisit the failed homes, the rooms,
the variously wrong devotions and decadences,
the waves you grasped rather than swimming.
Saying, whoever you are, it's mercy.

EXCERPTS FROM A SECRET PROPHECY

"We are only lightly covered with buttoned cloth; and beneath these pavements are
shells, bones, and silence." —Virginia Woolf, *The Waves*

NOCTILUCENT

"Not only all the dawns of summer—, not only
how they change themselves into day and shine with
    beginning.
Not only the days . . .

[. . .] For each of you had an hour, or perhaps
not even an hour, a barely measurable time
between two moments—, when you were granted a sense
of being. Everything."

—Rainer Maria Rilke, "The Seventh Elegy," *Duino Elegies*, translated by Stephen
Mitchell

JOANNA KLINK is the author of *They Are Sleeping, Circadian*, and *Raptus*. A recipient of awards and fellowships from The Rona Jaffe Foundation, Jeannette Haien Ballard, Civitella Ranieri, and The American Academy of Arts and Letters, she lives in Missoula, Montana.

EXCERPTS *from a*

SECRET PROPHECY

Also by Joanna Klink

RAPTUS

CIRCADIAN

THEY ARE SLEEPING